HOLDING

PATTERNS

UNIVERSITY OF PITTSBURGH PRESS

Published by the University of Pittsburgh Press, Pittsburgh, Pa., 15260

Feffer and Simons, Inc., London
Manufactured in the United States of America

Library of Congress Cataloging in Publication Data

Nathan, Leonard, 1924–
   Holding patterns.

   (Pitt poetry series)
   I. Title. II. Series.
PS3564.A849H6   811'.54   81-16163
ISBN 0-8229-3454-X   AACR2
ISBN 0-8229-5336-6 (pbk.)

Thanks are due to the Guggenheim Foundation whose support gave the author the leisure to begin this book.

Acknowledgment is made to the following publications for permission to reprint some of the poems that appear in this book: *Anthology of East Bay Poets, The Berkeley Monthly, Berkeley Poetry Review, Bits, The Blue Hotel, California Monthly, The Chowder Review, Cincinnati Poetry Review, Hawaii Review, New England Review, Plainsong, The Poetry Miscellany, Poetry Northwest, Practices of the Wind, Salmagundi, The Sole Proprietor,* and *Windflower Almanac.*

"The Fourth Dimension" originally appeared in *The Georgia Review.* "Altamira" and "View from the Mid-Fifties" are reprinted from *The Massachusetts Review,* copyright 1979 and 1980 by The Massachusetts Review, Inc. "News from the Low Country" and "Song" first appeared in *The Nation,* copyright 1979 by The Nation Associates. "Spirit" was originally published in *The New Yorker,* copyright 1978 by The New Yorker Magazine, Inc. "Airs" was first published in *The Ohio Review.* "Morning Song," "Leavings," "A Very Forgiving Person," "Hello Again," "Portrait," and "Cold Snap" are reprinted from *Prairie Schooner* by permission of the University of Nebraska Press. Copyright © 1979, 1980, and 1981 by the University of Nebraska Press. "Recognitions," "Seed," "The Affair," and "The Missed Beat" are reprinted by permission of *San Jose Studies.* "Last Watch" first appeared in Volume 6, #1 of *The Spirit That Moves Us* magazine, Iowa City, summer 1981.

*The publication of this book is supported by grants
from the National Endowment for the Arts
in Washington, D.C., a Federal agency,
and the Pennsylvania Council on the Arts.*

For Babette Deutsch

CONTENTS

CONTENTS

CONTENTS

I

The Given

THE UNDERSTANDING

We don't speak the same language
but by some miracle understand each other.
I hold up a pencil and say pencil
and you say yes, yes, pencil
and make signs of writing in the air
and the air becomes intelligible.

We don't need a translator to confuse us.
I look out at the sunset and say O
and you nod, yes, yes, yes
and maybe see the same vermilion
mingled with silver mingled with lemon,
cobalt with fire, earth with water.

You say perhaps we're speaking some
third language in a dream and it's all
illusion. We should pinch each other
to see if it's true. We pinch. It hurts.
We are nevertheless unconvinced.
We gossip. We abandon talk of the truth.

This becomes habit. We don't listen
anymore. We don't need to. I pinch you
now and then and can't remember why
and you cry out and we make up
and there are children around us like waves
tripping our feet. Do you understand?

I point to the sunset but you study the saucepan.
Yes, you say, I understand. The stringbeans
are about ready. Put out the wine.
I put out the wine. It doesn't matter
if it's not real. Language is just
music to live by anyway.

A MUSICAL OFFERING

Bach is spreading softly down
from the small house with one lit window
halfway up the hill.

I'm merely passing but stop and listen
with head bowed as one who receives the overflow
of another man's blessing.

It reminds me that the poor still wait
out in the rain, silently bearing their lives
like a burden of useless wings,

and that long dead stars send
waves of light out to the edge of darkness
though no one may ever see,

and that Bach himself, late and alone,
laying aside his towering wig, must
sometimes have stared blindly
into the candle.

MEADOW FOAM

Woe to them that are consoled . . .
—Marie Lenéru

The afternoon
hundreds of blackbirds
suddenly sprang up
out of the cedars of the cemetery
he felt, for Christ's sake,
a vision had been vouchsafed
the wrong man again,
as in that dry Mexican spring
when one sunset slowly spread
like a vast pang for the loss
of a whole heaven of light,
which he resented, knowing
that dust makes gorgeous
the banal glow of dying suns,
dust, our own poor medium,
or on that cold day in Normandy
when he alone met Evil,
a German tank half in a ditch
beside the road, its black cross
scorched, its long gun pointed
blindly at the milky sky,
and eastward, brown smoke
on the ghostly horizon, signaling
a great work in progress
of which he was a part but not
a part, or on that summer night
seated under constellations
of lit crystal when everyone
seemed moved together inward
by one concentric music, and then
applause fading into departure
like a tide going out

or exile into the dark
of yourself, and now this big
stagey uprush and whisper of flight,
a poor man's phoenix dissolving
before his very eyes, and he
stupidly as ever
disappointed and disappointed
with much else—"disappointed,"
a word pronounced like falling
down stairs, and here he was
at the bottom, unhurt, perhaps
a little stunned, grateful
for small bruises and—disappointed
because wars, election, views
of the Alps, of skyscrapers
and Rembrandts promised more,
and these flagrant visions
that seem to hint of Great Doings
behind the masks of mere light
and shadow, behind flesh (dust
again) and its best wishes, and here
he stood looking for a word
that would let him be—say, "reconciled,"
spoken with good-humored sadness
that made him feel like the ghost
of himself, one of the liberal dead
ready to accept anything almost,
even love, another distraction
from blackbirds and far-off figures
of glory, and without thinking
he turned to the woman beside him,

slender, tall almost
as he, a lilac scarf
around her gray hair that hung
in thin bangs across her forehead,
and the same gray eyes he'd watched
this morning as she studied her face
in the mirror, eyes not warmly open
as now, but narrowed, calculating
as a painter's, working only with flesh,
shadow, light, and a few pastels
to make a decent likeness
of her best self, the one
that accepted what was there
and what was not, seeing herself
maybe as simply the exposed negative
of a woman long gone
in the mirror, the lost and real one
he loved, as she herself loved
the far-off man whose decent likeness
she now smiled at, reconciled
and disappointed and there's your love
for you, the fine art of charity
and tact, of noticing and not
noticing, for example, people,
the world, or little scenes in it
like the modest arrangement of cedars
out there, a good picture
of middle-class composure,
their shade obscuring gravestones,
names, dates, woes of the flesh,
hopes, disappointed love,

and making death into a tame
old pasture missing only
its pious white mare and her
sleepy aura of flies, or making
life a kind of exclusive club
for self-pity, civil doubt,
and guilt, a private place to think
occasionally of those excluded—
beggars on Bombay streets asking
for nothing more than another day
like the last, black-eyed children
watching enemy jets scream in
over low white buildings,
his neighbor, a strong old man
with a bad heart, and so on
till he cried (without moving
his lips), "Not this, not this!"—
but what then, what? and was answered
by his own heart beating hard
as though caught sleeping on duty,
the same old faithful pump
fifty-eight years serving it knew
not what, perhaps the vague hunger
they used to call the soul,
a sort of dumb cry and flutter
in the dark or cave of dreams,
unique all right, but over
the long haul nothing special,
nothing to interest the Great Powers
of Light and Darkness, yet knowing
itself caged in the wrong world,

trying hard to remember back
to some translucent first cause
or ahead to a radiant last one
but always getting stuck in details,
say, the manner in which light
(lower-case illumination)
defines a soft curve of flesh
out of mere shadow to become
a whole strange dependable face
in the chill frame of pure silver,
or the way common blackbirds crash
into an almost acceptable scene
to distract the comfortably disappointed
from their little faith,
or even simpler, as when she knelt
last Saturday morning by the sea,
knelt at what he hadn't noticed
just at his feet, a white surprise
or wild flower out of its place,
time, maybe even its world,
knelt of a sudden and said softly
over it its local name
which he had forgotten till now, and now
repeated like an unanswerable prayer
for all things that must stand for themselves,
things plain to the vision—
repeated without moving his lips,
"meadow-foam, oh meadow-foam,
of course," and that would have to do.

TABLE TALK

Therefore, this first kind of grace, common to all, is seldom called grace.
—Erasmus

She was just about to say,
through the candles and over the wine,
with the oak table and so much else
between them, that distance
was no less fine an invention
than the wheel, but didn't
because his smile was too far off,
so asked softly instead: Are you there?
and knew, though he lifted his glass
to her, he wasn't, but somewhere back
in himself alone with something dearer
to him than any woman now,
what—for modesty—he called
his disappointment, that is, failure,
which these days left her much
to herself to decide just who
she was after all these years
typecast as daughter, wife, mother,
double agent in the lost war
of the sexes, or someone yet to meet,
like the skeleton lady who wore *her* rings
in the mirror of a bad dream, or even
the limber unbespoken girl
she had betrayed centuries ago,
the same happy bird-boned fool
who used to float up through wild flowers
under pure wind music overhead
to reach a vision of the Bay below
where light was a shatter of green brilliants
so fierce she had to turn aside
and found there, like a consolation,
the pasture easing down at her left,

made comely by the pious grazing
of one dusty old roan and,
O Lord, gravity seemed with her then,
and when *he* arrived on the crest,
magnetism and also—touching—
electricity, and later darkness
seemed only an ample room for whatever
love, conjuring with small lights
or stars, could conceive in the sweet silence
of birds and all she had to do
was stretch out her hand and . . .
here she was now as though flushed
from a leafy drowse in which someone
had invented distance and it was real,
a kind of exile where she felt herself
diminished and solitary, observed
by an eye far off and detached
and nothing to do but sadly take
her helpmate's hand and walk off
into the thorns and thistles
and here they were finally, all
but alone—good gray tenants
of a nicely appointed future, complete
with this intimate candle fiction,
these artful wine-dark shadows
which softened disappointment and made
waiting for unthinkable death (she blushed
at that) a comfort that left him
the leisure to stare, as he did now,
right through flesh and blood
as though something waited further on,
some (of course) modest grail hidden

behind a misty door ahead, or perhaps
he saw nothing or the worser nothing
beyond nothing, or perhaps distance
was for him a place you were duty-
bound to visit from time to time,
like the cemetery they strolled
this afternoon to call on old friends
and were both shaken by a wild upflutter
of blackbirds in their hundreds
that left him gaping at the radiant void
of their absence (much, she thought, like a cow
gazing rapt at a spot where something
strange had passed) and she wanted to take
his hand—helpmate, old companion—
and tell him she also could see
immense prospects narrowed to one
beige accoustical tile
of an institutional ceiling, and so
to trust neither in visions nor dreams,
but in faithful seeing or trying to see
just what was there or almost there
(things flapped off so fast), as one
absolute time she saw, as she looked
over the water below, saw and accepted,
perhaps a mile out, a small
white sail leaning far over
the green dissonant swells, folding
the wind to its own purpose
like a sheer garment, not hers
and not her purpose but near enough
to see the free uses of grace
and the fair chance of such small

impromptu choices as sailors are given,
though it was now he who leaned forward
and asked: Are you there? and she wanted to add
that this woman or disappointment
across the table from him and like him,
was an outlandish specimen, creature
from alien space or long distance
arrived to discover what was human
or left after the romance of visions,
dreams, failure, and common
household pain, but answered instead
unsmiling: Yes, I'm here (where else
on earth could she be!) and lifted her glass.

THE MISSED BEAT

You've heard that pause
in summer when crickets skip
a beat, as though the earth
were shifting to a new rhythm
that only things pressed to its pulse
would detect and adjust to.

Somewhere back in the forties
I must have missed a shift,
being in the city much
where crickets are kept out
by ordinance, a steady traffic
of noise clear through sleep.

Anyway, my steps
since have been a little off,
my balance poor. These nights
I listen to that country music
to get the time again
to move the way I must.

HOMING

There are still some trails
that follow so far under fir shadow
you can still hear yourself breathe —
between two clear syllables of water —
the one word, simple
as moss, for belonging forever
just where you are.

In the city, birds
make a different adjustment, telling
each other: "This is not home,
this shrill and smoky branch, but a place
to fly from, one of many
possible selves." And that's
what we call singing.

NEAR THINGS

for Carol

The wild blackberries I gathered that morning
when the world seemed on the lit verge
of some especially lovable form
were still bitter. You smiled anyway.
It was your second-best smile,
the one reserved for making do
with things as they are, and we did.

And as the day slowly ripened,
everything we saw or touched
touched us in consolation
for a sweetness we never had—and it was good.
That night the stars were simply
beyond reach and we ignored them
for this world, dark as it was.

TOAST

There was a woman in Ithaca
who cried softly all night
in the next room and helpless
I fell in love with her under the blanket
of snow that settled on all the roofs
of the town, filling up
every dark depression.

Next morning
in the motel coffee shop
I studied the made-up faces
of women. Was it the middle-aged blond
who kidded the waitress
or the young brunette lifting
her cup like a toast?

Love, whoever you are,
your courage was my companion
for many cold towns
after the betrayal of Ithaca,
and when I order coffee
in a strange place, still
I say, lifting, this is for you.

II
News from the Low Country

CONVERSATION PIECE

Of late I've been talking to my shadow
more and more. Why not? He's read Pascal
and Buber. He's lain awake nights thinking
through the Great Questions, above all
the existence of the soul, which you and I
had thought a dead issue. He's not so sure.

Simensky, I say (that's his name), you're
a reader, a philosopher, so tell me—when
the lights go out, when all that's left is fear,
a snuffle like horses, the sudden silence of crickets,
when footsteps walk into the middle of sleep
and stop as if in thought, what then are dreams? Dreams?

Simensky, your silence on this matter suggests
that experience, this bare handful of water,
sometimes sweet, sometimes stale, matches
my thirst so well, that I may really be meant
for this world, period. The rest is—oh—
shadow calling out to shadow, absence to absence.

We go on like this until it's dark
when my mooning lamp gives Simensky
an especially soft look as though he wanted
to console me for being so obscure. Simensky,
I whisper, this breathing, is it the truth,
the whole truth? He nods and reaches for the bottle.

THAT THE UNEXAMINED LIFE
IS NOT WORTH LIVING

So, butterfly,
you and the leaf you sit on—
bronze idling on bronze—
are just going to have to die
without knowing how pretty
and pointless your lives are.

We humans, however,
understand the backward grace
of flight and fall, and also
understand the pity
of not knowing, and also
the pity of knowing.

THE SISTERS

All the girls who have ever been hurt
and are yet to be
can hear the cries of a girl
being just now hurt
though they pretend not to.

They are like the trees in a forest
where the echo of one axe
roots them deeper in their own pain,
sisters of silence, every leaf
the same unspeakable word.

Down where the stone's cold shadow
moves on the calm face of ditchwater
everyone tells the truth, a small thing
but it makes being here like nothing else—
no love quite like hunger,
no hue like gray, no music like breathing,
no kindness so tender as the soft
reception of a homeless leaf.

HOMEBODY

She sent her steps out
every day to find the clean edge
of her life. They came back dusty
and tired with a long story
of one path leading only
to another and on and on.

She sent her eyes out
traveling the speed of light
toward the romance of the horizon
and they came back bloodshot at dusk
peering in at the window, afraid
to look into her hopeful sockets.

She sat in the dark waiting
for word from the past or future
to make the present happen,
praying now, now, but already
it was too late. She set her watch
by grass and went under.

SNAPSHOT OF ME AS A BOY

I'm lonely in the ashen field
as an abandoned shack is lonely
but doesn't know it.

It's the last honest age, a depression
of mild and pallid silence, years
before the lie of color.

You others who ran after time
hoping to reach the present,
see what you've missed?

Not one gray leaf fallen,
not a single black rose
of the hedge blown.

SEATING ARRANGEMENT

Every time the teacher looked up,
she saw you shining in the first seat,
me behind you and so on, back
to the very back where he sneered,
a slump of bones and acne, the boy
who kept a secret in his chest—
TB.

He was last seen beside a gas pump
in Tarzana while you went on to one
good marriage after another,
sometimes in the *Herald* smiling
in black and pearls the rich news
of love, your hair as blonde as always,
maybe blonder.

I was the slow boy who worried,
is worried even now by what the teacher
had in mind when she looked up
from the roll, removed her glasses and sighed,
seeing us all as part of one
pronounceable thing. That's the lesson
I never learned.

PORTRAIT

Mother as a young girl
sixty years back, fair
daughter of hope, helpless
as an apple blossom, now
dead, now studied by
the granddaughter who looks
most like her and sees
in that face the face
of a little sister who still
has to learn the facts of life.

Now, the boys cry,
O now!—but the next thing
she knows, her bed is falling
through moths and layers of shadow
each more black—mother,
sister, soul, O soft
little mouth opened
to the mute zero of wonder.

ANOTHER PURPOSE

You asked: what are we to do?
I stood by the window
looking out over the world
trying to avoid the answer
of distance.

Everything out there
wore the habit of solitude,
houses, buildings, the works
of man, quiet
as a cemetery.

I don't know. Each day
fewer words seem to explain,
or a simple gesture,
like you closing your eyes
as I talk.

Some evenings, looking out,
I feel called and turn
only to find it's supper again
and another purpose
is merely accomplished.

SPITTING IMAGE

Mr. Edelman, ex-tailor, socialist,
and seventy-six-year-old orphan,
sits by the blind window of dusk
fantasizing again in the coughed-out air
of the rest home, this time piecing together
a real man, himself as he should have been
given another world, and what pieces
he works with!—odds and ends of his own life,
hope, for example, and a faded passion
for a great purpose he can't remember now,
and the memory—brown as an old photo—
of a father bearded and swathed in the dark habit
of foreign wisdom and lost occasions. And then,
the last remnant of all is outrage that sometimes
rings in his ears like high blood pressure
and has to serve these final days as proxy
for an old-fashioned soul. And it's now the doctor
finds him adrift in the dark, playing again
with himself, and bends to call his name
till he looks up with the eyes of someone else,
a proud demented alien with a smile
to match, which straightens the doctor up, and then,
for godsake, the old boy spits and spits again,
and the doctor, smiling, calmly explains to the nurse
how the senile often retreat to the child's first
unreasonable rage and spitting may only be
a crude negative form of need and besides
(he hopes to himself, as he wipes the froth off his tie)
the old fart can't hang on much longer,
but Mr. Edelman is hoping otherwise
in a kind of prayer that goes something like this:
If not happy then maybe brave, and if
not brave then loving a little, and if not that
so a good story to tell the children.

MORNING SONG

Dreaming the actual world,
I saw you again last night,
the moon turning your dark hair
its own color, your face the face
of my first girl, a fantasy
full of bitterness and hope,
nothing on earth more beautiful.

If they ask who you are, I'll say,
sister of death, cold daughter
of wishes only come true
in the risen Atlantis of sleep, and yet
most constant of all, waiting
at the missed stations ahead, patient
as love, for what I'll never be.

YES, BUT

Something
persists even through the smoky ritual
of autumn dusk when you receive
as a present for resignation
a valuable gold sunset
to keep time by.

Something
that won't rest even
in your sleep, that regards
the just work of a lifetime
as a mere distraction
from serious business.

Something
that has the address of a place
you've never been to, and paces your garden
bitterly planning its next move
but does not know the name
of the simplest flower.

Something
that was before and will be after,
ghost maybe or unborn child
of some insatiable love or illusion of love
that wanted everything,
all your life, your death.

ALTAMIRA

In this dream or cave is a deeper cave
as in this dreamer is another man
painting a man holding a spear, running
across the rock face after or away
from something—darkness, footsteps, animal breathing.

He wants to waken but wakens every time
into a bigger cave or dream of running,
the same man with the same spear painted
across the rock face, waking or dreaming
as it was, is, and always will be.

GHOSTS

I often think ghosts
are of the living
who have lost that part of themselves
that can't pass through.

Sadness always gets through
and sometimes a certain levity,
and a great yearning to touch, but touch
never gets through.

INTENSIVE CARE

for Julia

Someone begins to sing faintly
in the wan blue night of the ward,
someone hanging by four thin tubes
from a steel rack like a gallows.

The duty nurse cocks her head.
It could, of course, only be breathing,
breathing become a sort of song
and maybe that's what it is.

She herself has often awakened
from work and caught herself humming,
a thoughtless little anthem of being
for its own pure sake.

It sets her thinking slowly back
to her own girlhood—O little bird,
little white bird!—and she wants to cry,
grateful for no good reason.

She rises lightly now and, gliding
down the numb aisles of sleep,
all around her hears faint breathing
like a dim feathery chorus.

III

Near Relations

SEED

You have your reason
for planting it and it
has its reason for growing.
If there are any other reasons
the burden for their proof
is on the conscience of angels
and if its color is almost
the color of your own flesh
don't be fooled.

                    This
is not about the lowly
miracle of persistence
and certainly not about love,
though if it were, it would also
and especially have to be
about loneliness and death,
but no, it's about one brief
unscrupulous victory.

HOLDING PATTERN

for Somebody's Old Aunt

A dream: she is learning to fly
without wings. Well, nonsense,
but what isn't these days?—
thus when the mocking bird
wakes her (never so fine
in its mocking as now and never
so much itself either),
she lies there and listens unmoved
by its intimation of something
rarer than it, a high-toned
golden nightingale
from a Chinese fairy tale
where there is no time
like the present, no arches
fallen, joints inflamed,
no cold oatmeal to rise to,
no need to escape
by the same street to the same
park to the same bench,
to waste the day in the shadow
of shakey elm leaves
stained with stale atoms
of smoke, to be cooed at
by pigeons, chirped at by her own
gray kind, and, home again,
cackled or crowed over
by her ruffled niece, and served
(whatever they call it) oatmeal,
and then to outwait night,
straining her watery glasses
over some birdbrained romance,
and then to sleep, to dream,

perchance to fly, and fall
back into the world
only to wonder if rising
again is not merely
to yield to the bad habit
of hope, but now hears
the mocking bird insist
with its whole gray soul
that morning calls for some
sort of celebration,
even if what you sing
is someone else's solo,
a mocking anthem of joy
which demands that she rise again,
wingless and doubtful as ever,
rise and warily open
the blinds expecting as ever
to find only what's there
and sees, like a shy vision,
that at least the anxiety
of the poplars is no longer
her anxiety, that the blue
and innocent emptiness of the sky
is not her emptiness
and so (humming without knowing
she hums) washes her body,
removing from it what wastes
she can, robes herself
in something clean and simple,
then wambles down the stairs,
flat step by flat step,
to honor the oatmeal with honey

and abide the bitterness
in the plucked souls of her kin,
caged as she is in the wrong
and only life as only
she among them knows,
now entering the kitchen
warm as a new-laid egg,
the first human, the first
always to rise, thinking
that this dream, stranger
than all, will soon be over,
but I'm having it now,
so it's mine, of my making
or mocking, homely bird,
poor man's nightingale,
and lifts like a toast the first
sweet adequate mouthful.

JUBILEE

Listen—she's coming now
through the long sigh of a bus door,
through the weepy gusts
of November, up the twilight boredom
of twenty-seven (count them) steps,
and now into the room where the light
suddenly remembers things
just as they were this morning,
though lonelier perhaps
and that could be why she flings
her hood back as if in defiance
and, muttering, peels off her raincoat
like an old skin, hanging it high
to shed the tears she won't,
and why she charges the kitchen,
surprising the absence out of it,
to start the kettle heating,
and only then comes back out to drop
with a sigh into the giving
old armchair where bitterly
she recalls she's stopped smoking
again so, damn it, there's nothing
to do before she warms the leftovers
but quietly be
here between the day's petty rages
still pecking in her skull
like a typewriter, and the night's
long well-read solitude yet to come,
for she expects no one and hasn't
for thirty years since she packed
her girlhood in the trunk
with all the innocent trash of memory
and her mother's wedding dress,
which is only to say

she trails neither glory
nor dust behind her and owes the future
nothing but next month's rent
so she can sit in the calm pasture
of this moment and summon back,
atom by weary atom,
her scattered self into that simple composure
which is also the wholeness or beauty
of otherwise homely queens
in their full power, the very thing
we've been waiting here
to tell her all this time,
but in her kingdom have no more mouth
for it than ghosts and anyhow
she doesn't believe in ghosts,
only in what remains after the trunk
is locked, which for her, it seems,
is a chronic procession of small erasable choices,
like being just or kind
from one faithless moment to the next,
choices you wouldn't notice
unless you cared to,
and now, changing
into a blowsy red robe,
she hears the kettle commence
its hysterical jubilee
and by God thinks
tonight she'll have brandy before sleep,
the imported kind that begets
such smooth experienced fire
out of mere sweetness and time,
to be served in her place only
on proud occasions of state.

THE NEWS

My mother's voice
before the last stroke,
sang so lightly, I thought
she was just happy for once
or had some girlish secret
she couldn't confide
except in code: a fall
broken to me like good news.

Mother?
Mother, is that you?

No, it's a sparrow
or spirit occupying
the same space I am—
they can do that, you know.

And then it all seemed clear
as one occupying spirit
telling another exactly
the way it feels down here.

THE CALLING OF MR. BAILEY

For life is a dream a little less inconsistent.
—Pascal

If God ever speaks to Mr. Bailey,
it should be on a night like this—
a pit of black silence containing
only the distant bark of a dog,
his wife's hoarse breathing beside him,
the sciatica grinding deep in his hip,
and this waiting for light so he can rise
and wait for dark on the front porch,
watching the same children head
for the same school, the same shadow
of the same mailman ripple over
the same hedge, the same bees
in the same honeysuckle and the same
brief snooze and same weariness
to wake yawning in the same world
so it hardly mattered whether his eyes
were open or shut and maybe it all
was the same dream of a dull dreamer,
someone just like him—retired,
an old sack of dusty miseries
and small purposes, and nothing to say
after all those years—explaining the silence
but not why the bed suddenly trembles,
though that's because his wife chooses now
to rise up slowly, pale
as a phosphorescent fish gliding
under fathoms of unlit water
on her way, he guesses, to urinate,
and then back again, settling
dark into darkness beside him, eerie
and still creature unto itself,
as they all are and he feels, my God,

abandoned in a blackness peopled
by pulsing blue lights, spirits
fluttering like fish or moths and he
the sole flesh-and-blood human,
sciatica and all, as though he'd retired
not just from his old job,
but from the world, and wants to cry
because it's the truth, when he hears a voice
call, "Bailey, Bailey," and stares around
to find himself now in a bus station
big as a cathedral, the travelers
vague as moths through gray and shadow
and the voice commanding, "Listen, Bailey,
they're all actually singing and someone
has to hear them!" and so he hears them
under a vast invisible dome,
every song unto itself
but part of a huge music whose words
he can only a little understand,
something about a vineyard, a tower,
a winepress, but the hope in it
is too much; and he starts to cry
as though drunk with elation but knows
he's dreaming because the pain flows in
right through sleep, loud as the music
in which every voice is beloved
or loving if only heard right
and he too wants to sing but the voice
is calling again, "Bailey, Bailey,"
and he turns in the dark, his eyes wide,
and is touched by his wife as she mutters,
"Bailey, you're talking in your sleep,"

but the tears are still wet on his face,
the sciatica still singing, and this joy,
this sweet hysteria in his chest,
is still alive so it's all right
because if God will not speak,
he, Bailey, has plenty to do,
a new job, the hardest ever—
to see and hear as never before,
Bailey, the night watchman for dawn
and listener for secret music, who,
when the time comes, will rise and take
his seat as a fresh witness to the creatures
out there trying to be something more,
a whole people or nation of music,
and failing, stunned by the gong of pain,
by other voices, or shut solitary
in darkness but singing on anyway
in the dim vineyards or stations of sleep,
singing without knowing they sing,
even now as daybreak flares
like light faintly through a glass dome
in which he too is an only voice,
but hears that other voice again
cry, "Bailey, wake up, you're at it
again!" and he is and he doesn't care.

SOLEMN MUSIC

Especially in rain my faith
is with women talking on the other side
of a wall, sometimes low and in sorrow,
sometimes laughing without reason,
a music almost becoming words.

Of course, I'd rather believe
like you in the long green trill
of a bird, or the root mystery
of a dead tree that can blossom
a man, or simply in the facts.

But rain persuades me that nothing
will last but the low voices of women
reciting sorrow inside, hymning
unreasonable joy while they wait for me
to enter and join their secret devotions.

THE SERVANT OF STARS

When she took the whiskey sours out
of his hands, Dawn, the new
cocktail waitress, whispered to Jack,
the aloof bartender, that he looked
a lot like Humphrey Bogart, his back
to the world, and frowning as though distracted
by the smoky violet mirror
that spanned the whole length of the bar
like a cold and darkling window on
to space in which faint constellations
with common names like Mary, Bud,
and Doc were composed of little lights
you may have thought were only human—
glint of eyes leaning forward
to drink, flash of a wedding band,
gleam of an earring, cigar glow—
a galaxy Jack could now observe
like some alien disguised as one
of *them,* say Humphrey Bogart, so
that when he turns to face the world
things are not the same, flushed
with a dim radiance that fringes
even the same old stunts:
Bud's sadness that held out
to the fifth Scotch, Mary's refusal
to take money for what she swears
is love, Doc's boyish grin
while his bony hand squeezes the throat
of his glass, and finally Jack himself,
his heart beating from sheer habit,
his hairpiece turning gray with worry,

his wife lost, taking with her
hope like the child they never had,
and here he is again suddenly
feeling—what? Space Sickness?
or maybe Space-Time sickness,
a queasy passion to tell them all
the terrible news of desolation,
of black distances that no one
can ever cross, and how they drink
their own pity . . . but instead
he swabs the bar, pretending to wait
for the next order, pretending to be
Humphrey Bogart coolly noting
Dawn move off across the room
on brave skittish legs ready
to take a long run at time,
awkward and graceful both, as only
the young can be, her brown hair
lambent as candle light, her eyes,
turning back to him, him,
encouraging she knows not what—
the wrong man, poor double
for a dead star, himself simply
a poor double for something no one
ever saw, and now—what's this?—
Jack smiles at her a little
idiot smile the mirror cannot
see but the bar can, glaring
darkly up with a different version
of his face as though the heart
of wood opened to show him still

another secret self to hide from,
and he buries it beneath the rag
and vows never to ask which one
is real, if any is, and vows
further to do his job as if
that were all and composes himself
into the man he has to be,
a constellation of aches, rages
and fears, and this trifling skill,
all which answer to one name,
meaningless if said like a mantra
over and over, and yet, said once,
said only once a certain way . . .
O Jack, no more of that. Pity
but not love, drink but never
hope in this desolation. Still
(remembering her glance across
the whole length of the long room),
still there could be more to it
than *that*, something here unworldly
and clean that makes him stare out
over the bar as if at nothing,
but that's all right—no one, not
even she, notices because
these stars are so remote and blind.

IV
The Fourth Dimension

HELLO AGAIN

In every greeting a final goodbye is said.
That's why my hand fits so comfortably in yours
and why my eyes from the very first glance
have never stopped asking yours: when,
how, and for what good reason?

Every parting is a rehearsal for the last.
That's why you call up the stairs a second time
to tell me that this one is just for practice,
that you'll be back soon with cigarettes
and a newspaper full of fresh disaster.

Every life is an example of what to hope for.
That's why each morning the mirror is studied
with such dumb devotion like a page of scripture,
and why every new face is commentary
on the old testament of our own.

COLD SNAP

When the ice next comes down
over the taigas, the lakes, the northern cities,
the yellow shag of the wheat fields,
our eyes will open very wide
after thousands of years of sleep
to see the world again.

A smoky fire. On the cave wall
bisons stampeding south with spears in their sides,
taking with them the lost purpose
of our lives, leaving behind
a small pile of cold ashes
and a few cracked bones.

No one will have to ask—Who
am I? The stars will again shine down
on thin, clever, desperate companions,
reverent killers, moving wary
through the chill shadows and home will be
the word for anywhere.

VIEW FROM THE MID-FIFTIES

I fight the future with a squad
of small purposes, this chore
and that, weeding the garden, fixing
the sink, writing the poem.

These are my new heroes: the stone
for persistence, the moss for faith, the dead
for courage beyond the call of duty.
I fight on even in sleep.

One lapse of attention, the briefest
affair with the present and it's all over.
In dreams the future looks just like the past
seen through an empty socket.

FANTASIA

The old grand piano—
no one here can play it
or one can, but not well.
She's very shy.

Once I returned early and heard inside
a faltering little spray of notes.
But that was meant for her own soul
like a secret between sisters.

I coughed a little outside the door.
She pretended to be dusting.
When she ran the rag hard
over the treble keys

they yelped in pain.

The widower who perists in living on
with one bad lung and red roses,
watches her pass on the way home from high school,
her eyes always straight ahead, but the deer
that condescend to browse on the dark crowns
of his last passion often lift their eyes
to the flashlight with so pitilessly soft
a stare, his heart holds its breath every time.

Were she to turn just once, he knows he'd see
in her look the radical soul of a species
indifferent to isolated instances
of death or beauty, and his heart tells him—O
bitterly—these roses are meant for her.

THE CHOSEN

One morning a whole people
can wake up with nothing to do.
They look around fulfilled
and utterly without interest
at the promised land.

They stand listening before bushes
or incredulously tap rocks,
but the answer is always an echo
of their own making
or plain thirst.

Someone remembers to shout a command.
The women slowly get breakfast,
the men face outward,
searching the far dust,
looking for trouble.

SHELVING

for Andrew

A board, sanded smooth white
as the inside of a girl's thigh,
lies in the dark of the basement waiting
for screws, for stain, for varnish, and finally
the books that explain how one thing,
without even trying, becomes another.

SOMETHING HAPPENS AND

There's nothing left
except what you are
and that tugs insistently
downward toward the moth shadows
of sleep. Good morning!

You have been judged
perhaps before the first star
condensed into a point of light
you've followed for years
to this conclusion.

So here you are
dreamless at dawn, the one time
nothing is granted but hope.
The birds know this
and sing to start the world.

It starts—
a stiff back, a dry cough,
the smell of bacon, eyes
that open warily, the mirror
saying: that's it.

EXPLANATION

When you said it wasn't my fault
but something in you that you couldn't explain
I knew you were already a memory
I had of a girl who stood at the window
looking out on the lost freedom of distance.

All that's left is a white blouse
in the closet, like a schoolgirl who can't explain
why she wants to be left alone,
or like a younger sister hiding
from the predestined failure of grown-ups.

I wish I could comfort her with flowers
or a future full of the sweets she thinks
we've cruelly withheld, but it's you she needs,
you, to explain what it's like to be absent,
to be a memory that can't explain.

THE FOURTH DIMENSION

Some part of us lives
always in the fourth dimension,
the invisible part
which can pass through walls,
falls hopelessly in love with light
and asks us in bad dreams
what touching is like.

This is not the soul
or anything that God made,
only the imperfection or wonder
of something that can't be touched.
It looks out of Einstein's eyes
as innocence or sorrow
for a time never to be lived in.

A VERY FORGIVING PERSON

The rain has stopped. Hurt again,
she reinvents a face, holding it
up close to the hall mirror
for a last myopic look. Good!

And now it's time to clear out.
If he'd have left her one reason to forgive,
even, she adds with a witty sniff,
a bad one—but to hell with all that.

She sweeps her orange silk scarf
off the brass hook by the door and leaves
for the last time, as though a betrayal
had cleansed her of a dirty sorrow.

Down the street, dark glasses stroll
the fresh egg of the world, glittering
like rich Italians. She sparkles among them
in her white coat and clean fury.

She hears and rejects the birds. She swears
that love next time is going to pay
for its keep. She means business.
The birds sing on anyway.

RITES OF PASSAGE

This boy, no man
until he's speared his lion,
cannot believe that in some lands
there are no lions, only boys
wandering over the world
hunting their fathers.

LIGHTING UP

When she leaned forward
to light up from the candle's
little halo between us,
for that instant
her grave young woman's face
inflamed darkly like the face of a lover,
not mine.

And then her words restored
the world to its homely oppression
but not even the rich bitterness
of coffee could shake
my faith in that flame
and I envied a perfect stranger and feared
for him.

THE SCROLL

In this sleep an old Chinese,
thin as a willow leaf, drifts
into his misty hut.

We're with him now
as he sits at a small table.
We're the pain in his lower back,

the headache through which he sees
the scroll, the cold hand
unrolling it slowly.

We read the poem
he has brushed there, our own exile
elegantly set down.

We think of the waterfall,
the white vein on the far-off
blue cliff face,

of pines dripping, of the brown river
and the small boat tied
in its reeds. Listen.

We're going to cry
but pour ourselves a cup
of wine instead.

We think reality
is only the pain and the cold,
and wake up

cold, hurting in the same
old places, our dream
still with us.

AIRS

for Miriam

It was just another story:
my mother, a schoolgirl hurrying
by the deserted house,
heard a mandolin. The windows
were boarded up. Her eyes got big
with restored belief in the telling.

And now she's gone. Silence,
but not for long. Downstairs
my daughter is playing "Rustles
of Spring," another story
in which I hear a schoolgirl
believe in haunting music.

HUGGING

Hugging me after twenty years,
she was also hugging her own past,
begging its forgiveness
for the betrayal of every
lost hope—her bridal slimness,
her blue infinite future.

It seems I'm a vessel now
for the spoiled wishes of old friends.
I mean more to them than I do
to myself. I'm exalted, trapped.

DREAMERS

My great-grandfather in Kiev
couldn't have dreamed an Apache brave
any more than that same brave
could have dreamed
my great-grandfather.

I try hard these contemporary nights
to imagine those two discussing me
by a homely fire, their few words
weighty and slow, their heads
nodding in sad assent.

They take me for a bad dream
with no future, so I explain to them
civilization, its discontents,
its idea of brotherhood,
but they know what they know.

SO?

So you aren't Tolstoy or Saint Francis
or even a well-known singer
of popular songs and will never read Greek
or speak French fluently,
will never see something no one else
has seen before through a lens
or with the naked eye.

You've been given just the one life
in this world that matters
and upon which every other life
somehow depends as long as you live,
and also given the costly gifts of hunger,
choice, and pain with which to raise
a modest shrine to meaning.

V
Soundings

SPIRIT

I'm thinking now of something
sighted once, maybe,
on the gleaming floor
of January: a small creature
wary under fir branches,
every breath pulsing
its whole body like a shudder,
its purpose so plain and mysterious
you could stare all these years
and see only how suspect
was your first and surprised view
of the thing (whatever it was)
as a sorry sight, because
surely it filled its moment
as warmth fills anything
that wholly contains it, as joy
flutters unreasonably
in the same brutal cage
where the heart beats
merely to keep time.

LEAVINGS

The goldsmiths of Chimu
are beaten flat
under seven layers of rubble
and silence
but have left us a face
to put on death.

It's a mask of light,
a radiant and blind gazing up
with two white shells for eyes
and a slash of darkness for mouth
since there's nothing more to be seen
or said in this world.

That's all they saved
by their art,
a relentless staring back
up at the sun as equal
to equal, as gold beaten
flat until human.

DUTY CALL

If you've come to be kind
to Mrs. Bailey in her garden,
to patronize her violets,
praise her roses, inhale
the fragrant pity of her being
used and abandoned by men, by children,
and now even by the little flowers
she must kneel to for lack of love,
don't,
because she knows all this
by heart and knows too
under the mindful shadow of her sun hat
the whole dirty catalogue
down to the pure selfishness
of the least seed, and how spring
is incurable, involving one death
after another, and how her devotion
is going to be buried
every fatal time
with the compost, to rise again
so green and almost eager,
you might worry that she'll forget
and ask God or you something
impossible, but no—she won't
hope for more than one life
after another, not even hers,
or hers only to care
for what she can, say
this stray thistle
she studies a little
before looking up with the very smile
you've earned simply by meaning

almost well, the same assent
the postman simply accepted
when, passing this morning
he left her nothing, not even word
of a new weed killer, but now
she's got to attend aphids, my dear,
dandelions and this brown
mysterious grief in the junipers,
so goodbye and as you politely
back out, watch for the thorns.

THE AFFAIR

The old plum outside my window
has lost all but a few blossoms
this morning after a sweet merciless rain.

They say love is unworldly.
After all these years I don't know
what the world is. I imagine things.

I imagine a girl rising
like a dancer, pleased with her own body
as though it were a lovely young friend.

Now I imagine her eating breakfast,
seriously scanning the news by her plate,
a promising student of things as they are.

I imagine that to lose almost
every blossom and still imagine
something beautiful after is simply love.

Old plum, what are we anyway
but things as they are, persistent spirits
hopelessly in love with the other world?

LAST WATCH

Sometimes there's a lull in the long war
between Darkness and Light, as now, September,
a day like a roomful of just-departed cigar smokers.

On the park bench sits a perfect stranger
in an overcoat of soggy brown leaves
stuck together to fit someone bulkier and dead.

Wind teases his few pale hairs.
His hands sleep one on each knee.
His face is beaten mulberry red as though by tiny hammers.

It's the eyes that bear watching. They belong on the bridge
of a rusty trawler rolling in northern waters,
expecting no landfall. The orders: watch.

He watches. It's perhaps the last duty
of the soul, the curious animal that refuses to accept
the doctor's indulgent advice to die with its eyes shut.

What does he see? Something beyond Thule,
beyond brute ice slabs and radiant blue channels—
the purity of what's there only to see.

It shines for him. He sees. He does not need it.

SONG

Floating up the iron stairs
of the library stacks, a girl's small voice
softly singing "Deep Purple,"
followed by the girl herself clutching
to her breast a big volume
like a child in her bare arms
or a change of linen.

Her smile, as we passed, slowed my descent
a little to listen hard to that music
gliding down behind her, fluent
as a bridal train as she went higher
and higher into the silence of knowledge
above me and the book of my wonder
opened to a clean page.

WAITING ROOM ONLY

Death has a younger brother
who hates his success.
There are nineteen cases
coming for the doctor today
not counting himself and his nurse
whose impatient red hair
just won't stay pinned
under a sterile cap
so she has to brush back
a little flame from her eyes
as she begins in a voice
flat as Kansas
to toll each afflicted name
at its appointed hour
beginning with Mr. Bailey
who limps up ramshackled
in faded tans, a smile
on his baggy face, pocked
as a target, and you may now recall
(if you're the doctor and you are)
that this too was born
of woman, come forth like a flower
to be cut down at last
but until then to be treated
as though a life could go on
forever if only you keep
at it, as he keeps
at it, breath after breath,
hauling himself here
like a sack to be looked into,
though the first thing to fly out
is the mercy bird hope,
a white flutter around

84

your head that you have to ignore
listening to the old heart
do its job, as Bailey
did his fifty years
faithful as an ox marching
through mud, up one row,
down another and you want
to ask why, why and what
is it to be human, to be
faithful, marching blindly,
or, as you do now,
to listen, tap, feel,
and even think suddenly
of a sick old elm
cut down, but its stump
this spring anyhow
blindly shooting at the sun
dozens of green saplings—
stupid that you should feel
this clear defiance a witness
for your own dumb kind,
for Mr. Bailey smiling
among the ashes and dust
when he might be demanding why,
why of his miserable comforter,
but waits, patient as a hireling
for a petty wage, this prescription
for local pain and, grateful,
departs, leaving the nurse
alone with you a moment—
that burning strand almost
enough to make you forget
autopsies of what someone

loved too little or much,
or does its defiance remind you
of such half-witted transgressions
against necessity
and time, as the gladness
of Mr. Bailey, the passion
of a blind stump, testimony
you can't credit but is yet
hurtfully real, as she summons
(brushing a little fire
from her eyes) the next affliction
and you know then that the time
is already lost and has been
from the first hour and yet
you go on listening, feeling,
even thinking between
their troubles of one refusal
after another to give in,
as your patients refuse, however
meekly they enter and go,
as the elm refuses, coming
to light again, as you also
refuse to hate yourself now
for being of this kind,
miserable but unrepentant
among the ashes and dust,
getting set for the next grief,
jealous as a lover
for the least sign of life,
defeated into gladness
by one little fallen strand
of red hair or fiery
heartstopping refusal.

LISTENING TO GUNNAR EKELÖF

Gunnar Ekelöf says he heard—
or dreamed he heard and still hears—
wild geese high over the grounds
of the mental hospital.

Around him the patients shambled in slow
hysterical circles and, beyond the iron bars,
pastures smoked and pale red suburbs
went on forever under the fall dusk.

But here were these geese heading north
and his heart leapt. He knew then
that something buried in all this madness
was still lucid and untouched.

And suppose he was dreaming—isn't a dream
also a sort of proof? Have any
of you dreamed better? I never have.
I hear him high above still heading north.

REMINDER

It seemed to you that the bright stream
in the valley below was a silver ribbon
around the gift of a whole county,
wrapped in grass, a white horse
grazing in one corner.

Next Christmas when other presents
disappoint you, remember this,
offered just because you were there
to receive and still to be opened.

THE SOUNDINGS

A freight train rattles and jars through sleep
in the cold grayness just before dawn
and I come to wild attention like a drowsy engineer
on the last of his shift, hauling darkness
behind him car after empty car and see
ahead the small lights of the city hiding
among them the last station of this run
and suddenly, alone with a present so pure
and moving, I reach over and sound the whistle
once and again and again like a great conch shell
pronouncing a solitary exaltation
there's no response to, except perhaps the sun.

Shirley Kaufman, *The Floor Keeps Turning*
Shirley Kaufman, *From One Life to Another*
Shirley Kaufman, *Cold Country*
Ted Kooser, *Sure Signs: New and Selected Poems*
Larry Levis, *Wrecking Crew*
Jim Lindsey, *In Lieu of Mecca*
Tom Lowenstein, tr., *Eskimo Poems from Canada and Greenland*
Archibald MacLeish, *The Great American Fourth of July Parade*
Peter Meinke, *The Night Train and The Golden Bird*
Peter Meinke, *Trying to Surprise God*
Judith Minty, *In the Presence of Mothers*
James Moore, *The New Body*
Carol Muske, *Camouflage*
Leonard Nathan, *Dear Blood*
Leonard Nathan, *Holding Patterns*
Kathleen Norris, *The Middle of the World*
Sharon Olds, *Satan Says*
Gregory Pape, *Border Crossings*
Thomas Rabbitt, *Exile*
Ed Roberson, *Etai-Eken*
Ed Roberson, *When Thy King Is A Boy*
Eugene Ruggles, *The Lifeguard in the Snow*
Dennis Scott, *Uncle Time*
Herbert Scott, *Groceries*
Richard Shelton, *The Bus to Veracruz*
Richard Shelton, *Of All the Dirty Words*
Richard Shelton, *You Can't Have Everything*
Gary Soto, *The Elements of San Joaquin*
Gary Soto, *The Tale of Sunlight*
Gary Soto, *Where Sparrows Work Hard*
David Steingass, *American Handbook*
Tomas Tranströmer, *Windows & Stones: Selected Poems*
Alberta T. Turner, *Learning to Count*
Alberta T. Turner, *Lid and Spoon*
Chase Twichell, *Northern Spy*
Constance Urdang, *The Lone Woman and Others*
Cary Waterman, *The Salamander Migration and Other Poems*
Bruce Weigl, *A Romance*
David P. Young, *The Names of a Hare in English*
David P. Young, *Sweating Out the Winter*